How To Find All Missing Persons / Unsolved Cases. And Collect All Reward Offers. Volume XXXIX. THE CASE OF STUART SPEIES WHO SWAPPED WITH TOM PHILLIPS

DAVID GOMADZA

www.twofuture.world

How To Find All Missing Persons / Unsolved Cases. And Collect All Reward Offers. Volume XXXIX. THE CASE OF STUART SPEIES WHO SWAPPED WITH TOM PHILLIPS

Copyright © 2024 David Gomadza

All rights reserved.

Paperback ISBN: 9798328513500

How To Find All Missing Persons / Unsolved Cases. And
Collect All Reward Offers. Volume XXXIX. THE CASE OF STUART SPEIES
WHO SWAPPED WITH TOM PHILLIPS

DEDICATION

To a better future.

How To Find All Missing Persons / Unsolved Cases. And
Collect All Reward Offers. Volume XXXIX. THE CASE OF STUART SPEIES
WHO SWAPPED WITH TOM PHILLIPS

How To Find All Missing Persons / Unsolved Cases. And Collect All Reward Offers. Volume XXXIX. THE CASE OF STUART SPEIES WHO SWAPPED WITH TOM PHILLIPS

CONTENTS

How To Find All Missing Persons /
Unsolved Cases.
And Collect All Reward Offers. Volume XXXIX.
THE CASE OF STUART SPEIES WHO SWAPPED
WITH TOM PHILLIPS 1
Afterlife Conversation. 6

and The Court Of Creation.

The Killers.   36

How To Find All Missing Persons / Unsolved Cases. And
Collect All Reward Offers. Volume XXXIX. THE CASE OF STUART SPEIES
WHO SWAPPED WITH TOM PHILLIPS

How To Find All Missing Persons / Unsolved Cases. And
Collect All Reward Offers. Volume XXXIX. THE CASE OF STUART SPEIES
WHO SWAPPED WITH TOM PHILLIPS

ACKNOWLEDGMENTS

Tomorrow's World Order

How To Find All Missing Persons / Unsolved Cases. And
Collect All Reward Offers. Volume XXXIX. THE CASE OF STUART SPEIES
WHO SWAPPED WITH TOM PHILLIPS

How To Find All Missing Persons / Unsolved Cases. And Collect All Reward Offers. Volume XXXIX. THE CASE OF STUART SPEIES WHO SWAPPED WITH TOM PHILLIPS

BACKGROUND INFORMATION

The real Tom Phillips is alive his coordinates are
08983678902848519263890284189028458678092368902849678901238168928478906832486
Now they swapped with a one aotepers stuverw meaning this is his electromagnetic wave
number 89284689028367890285876281028938617890124006836789012851091 20] who said I can if you can but what can we do about these meaning children who were abandoned by a previous dad a one Robert stuverx who said I can if they all respect me if not then what

can I if you can but if they don't respect me then what can I do I will leave them with the next step father see how good he can be with them

[electromagnetic wave is it's 87898902846789078902867890123489012489867890283284190210]

He then took poison and drunk it and died leaving 3 boys with Robert stuverx who was a doggy policeman and fbi said if I can then what can I do and recruited him for a drill where he brings his step children to the drill for a price of the money and have fun with other police officer then when he did not appear now Tom phillips is called to stand for him but this Tom phillips said I have daughters and I might be unable to handle situations with boys so I have a look alike with boys he will stand for him instead of me so Stuart Speies came and stood in place of robert stuverx and Tom phillips with 3 adopted kids whose mother was polish called mareena now this is what happened on that day this new guy said I can but what if the boys are not prepared for what's to come I came to see and not to die okay I must be serious about this every time someone does not turn up someone dies

Identified as Stuart speies who said I can but if we can't then we can't be forced fbi drills have carried huge risks this father of these boys did not die in a drill I was there he died on the scene shoot in the head at close blank by Tom phillips that was an accident argued the real top phillips who said I am still suspended pending investigations then he looked around and said okay I guess even I don't have a choice but I want to stress that the fbi has performed the most dangerous drills ever resulting in 9 casualties out of only 28 that's so high that fbi should be investigated but they keep increasing the pressure Tom phillips said you can handle it he patterned him on his shoulder blade.

1. Background Tom Phillips.

2. Police hunting for fugitive Tom Phillips and his three children have received more than 70 tip-offs over the last three days, including "several credible reports", as their searches move focus.
3. Waikato police have today announced they are scaling back operations in the Marokopa area in their search, as part of an expansion into the surrounding areas.
4. And they have revealed they've received more than 70 "new reports of information" about the fugitive dad and his missing children.
5. Acting Detective Inspector Andrew Saunders said this action was planned as part of an ongoing investigation.
6. "The four family members have been missing since December 12, 2021, when their father took his children to an unknown location believed to be in western Waikato, within Marokopa or the surrounding areas.

....

7. This week, police announced an $80,000 reward for information about the Ember, Maverick and Jayda."

https://www.nzherald.co.nz/nz/missing-marokopa-family-waikato-police-scale-back-search-in-marokopa-for-fugitive-tom-phillips/4NJLGGFOENFVNOAYDLK6VV5CU4/#:~:text=The%20four%20family,Maverick%20and%20Jayda.

8. Background Stuart Speies

No information yet.

How To Find All Missing Persons / Unsolved Cases. And Collect All Reward Offers. Volume XXXIX. THE CASE OF STUART SPEIES WHO SWAPPED WITH TOM PHILLIPS

TOMORROW'S WORLD ORDER'S PERSPECTIVES

USE OF PREDEFINED AFTERLIFE PARAMETERS

These guide souls the moment it exist the human body on its journey to Yahweh the creator these define what to do and what to expect as you go to hell or heaven if a souk leaves earth it enters ozone orbit and instantly everything reboots for it to start a new phase of life after living the earth's body now what happens is that it enters the ozone orbit and a simply click caused by the sudden drop of pressure from -1186 to – 20 means the bottom shaft of the soul will lift rapidly and this pushes its back into the air higher than its head best example is a penguin but with real human legs and head just the shape now God created a life predefined program for them instead of asking what should I do and where should I go they instantly know from predefined stencils if you did well and talked most about God then heaven is for you if you did evil and talked more about the devil then the devil is yours now if we Ask what can be of humans without souks this is the answer dead forever your soul is you a new transformation to the electromagnetic waves life where you see Yahweh for the first time and praise him and wish you had seen him a long time ago because of his Majesty and will always be there forever now what are all these you may ask these are rules to be guided by in the creation court in short it has everything humans know about the judges and the presiding judge who will always be Yahweh and 84 angels surrounding the altar 28 high priests who always say Yahweh have mercy on humans and 74 smaller courts priests who always say Yahweh has mercy on humans and 96 princesses who say glory to Yahweh forever and ever amen we have 96 elders who always say if I can why he can't meaning if the devil can drink blood why can't Yahweh who created the devil and blood do the same now this is not the same as saying if the devil can kill why can Yahweh its more on professional grounds rather than challenging now if we look at the inside of the court we have 81 priests surrounding the altar who say Yahweh be merciful to humans but if they disobey you we put hem on trial for you and kill them for you almighty Yahweh inside this is a round circle where Yahweh sits and asks questions now if we look deep inside the court you will see that there are other things that resemble earth high courts like benches and chairs 10 times human sizes for the gods who are so enormous 2 are equal to 84 billion humans in size

predefined parameters for humans after death as in know what is inside is a large size of books the book of creation is among them with 108978678928367890123486789012458617890l1 pages and is divided into humans first then chapter for animals then a chapter for angles then a chapter for gods and a chapter for Joseph Yahweh's best friend and a chapter for Yahweh's best friend's wife Anna and a chapter for Yahweh's wife Catitighit and lastly a chapter for Yahweh and recently a chapter for davidgomadza as Yahweh's representative on earth marking the new beginnings starting in 2025

1. tell us who killed you
2. tell us what killed you
3. tell us why and who killed you
4. tell us why you died
5. tell us what could have been done and is not done
6. tell us what could be and why
7. tell is when this happened
8. tell us why this is so
9. tell us why this is so
10. what can be done to improve this

What does the book of creation say about davidgomadza David Gomadza is the first and last ruler to be appointed by Yahweh fir the next 25 billion years and will act as his representative on earth deciding cases and upholding his principles on earth and as such has been entitled to 489 trillion dollars in assets this number signifies eternity among humans and the beginning of a new Era chapter 78678928028938628418902876890183208678901234867890 18236

487289128610 Creation manual the new Era of new electromagnetic wave conduit signed and dated by Yahweh himself on 27may2024 at 237800 Yatime
creation.universe.ya.start.end.find.davidgomadza.ya.askya.ya

Ask.read.creation.manucreation.universe.ya.start.end.find.davidgoma askya.ya

Ask.rulesofthecourt.start.now.start
David Gomadza welcome the rules of court are guiding principles that tell you what to do and how to do it first you must always say I believe in the court of creation and I shall abide by he rules of this court and shall always do things according to the rules of this court in deciding the cases I am assigned to you must ask what can be done so that you know all your options before making choices the court system will make it easy to check files and ask the outcomes of the decision ask the court the final decision in any case.

THE AFTERLIFE CONVERSATION AND THE COUNCIL OF CREATION'S ANAYLSIS.

stuart speies
current coordinates are
0897898678902836987890284687890289184867890284 1384
at the cave in arizona above coordinates now skeleton and skull pierced top left side and hide opening left side his cell number is 08789028387654386 but working just made a call to a number in california1
0897898678902836987890284687890289184867890284 1384
it's stuart speies who died on 25 april 2023 instead if the target tom phillips currently at coordinates
0898786789023489028789028410238678904861852801 20 arizona restaurant

The real Tom Phillips is alive his coordinates are

08983678902848519263890284189028458678092368902849678901238168928478906832486

Now they swapped with a one aotepers stuverw meaning this is his electromagnetic wave number 89284689028367890285876281028938617890124006836789012851091 20] who said I can if you can but what can we do about these meaning children who were abandoned by a previous dad a one Robert stuverx who said I can if they all respect me if not then what can I if you can but if they don't respect me then what can I do I will leave them with the next step father see how good he can be with them

[electromagnetic wave is it's 8789890284678907890286789012348901248986789028328419021 0]

He then took poison and drunk it and died leaving 3 boys with Robert stuverx who was a doggy policeman and fbi said if I can then what can I do and recruited him for a drill where he brings his step children to the drill for a price of the money and have fun with other police officer then when he did not appear now Tom phillips is called to stand for him but this Tom phillips said I have daughters and I might be unable to handle situations with boys so I have a look alike with boys he will stand for him instead of me so Stuart Speies came and stood in place of robert stuverx and Tom phillips with 3 adopted kids whose mother was polish called mareena now this is what happened on that day this new guy said I can but what if the boys are not prepared for what's to come I came to see and not to die okay I must be serious about this every time someone does not turn up someone dies

Identified as Stuart speies who said I can but if we can't then we can't be forced fbi drills have carried huge risks this father of these boys did not die in a drill I was there he died on the scene shoot in the head at close blank by Tom phillips that was an accident argued the real top phillips who said I am still suspended pending investigations then he looked around and said okay I guess even I don't have a choice but I want to stress that the fbi has performed the most dangerous drills ever resulting in 9 casualties out of only 28 that's so high that fbi should be investigated but they keep increasing the pressure Tom phillips said you can handle it he patterned him on his shoulder blade but instantly his heart started beating up fast and he said is there anything I should know first before I start this drill no one answered secretly someone said you whinge so much it's depressing then secretly someone said he whinge like a bitch but does nothing for all that pay check you should ask how much is in his agent bank account they all looked at each other then he said 4 bill yes his for this work since age 18 now he start becoming nervous he realise now that fbi will never let him take that money alive as since the 70s no one has ever took a penny it's just sitting and growing and total is 8 trillion they all looked at each other and he said I earned it risk free and now it start to look like culling all the former ones are dying in accidents I noticed that when the assigned doesn't turn up its the lead who is the target I am here today because I don't die for anyone and instantly they brought 3 kids in front of him you are going to play daddy to these boys until their father arrives Robert is never on time then he said just for a little bit of time then I am out of this scary jungle I saw Maneater footprints I was a scout they keep saying tiger who heard or have seen a tiger?

He looked at everyone and cursed hard and instantly a number arrived code 867890284867890 that coiled and instantly he farted then squirted shit that he only looked down and said whose number but no one looked but something whispered and said the father of these that's you are choosing to die for say fbi owe me 4 billion dollars keep the money and go he looked lost and said what all that money and it said you can make more we should be starting there today and he said where and it said new place his father escaped they are planning to kill him using his kids so he show up for them but he said they ate not mine you kill them then you kill someone else's kids manslaughter charges on fbi and the press if they know will call for the head of the fbi leader I am out I never come back fbi has become a terrorist group now getting innocent women and kids killed I lost mine my boy and girl but then I thought it was an accident I could not believe that fbi can be a risk to kids so I quit.

As soon as pc robert stuervx said I quit he remembers his children getting killed in a friendly cross fire where he mistaken his friends kids as his and relaxed and said mine are safe and sound there until a one Darren said they are mine check again at this point the kids had been under water for ten minutes crying for help as the oxygen musk had failed them only to find one still alife just waiting to die in his arms ever since he had refused to participate the fbi had heard that he was leaving leaving his account with 890876231 with the fbi as agent sturvex if he asks then they will look into withdrawals but this is the truth the fbi will never touch this money its to fight the future unknown if the wanted to be fair they could arrest all these agents and put them in jail but this move attracts the press who will start demanding to know about this case so he thought about and cried and last night changed and started working at a ranch called once we were heroes now forgotten then something rose up and said for now they will call you let all accidents happen when you are not there he smiled.

I an robert stuverx but people call me robert sturvex but I think it's the same until I want to withdrew my 4 billion dollars with the fbi money I thought I could have one day but which I am sure they will never release the money for as I find out it's to fight a supervillain to come who has powers of the gods to know everything just by looking at things that's scary but my money full stop Pc aopqrstop meaning astopqrstuvw standing for monopqerst arranged the drill and threaten to blow the kids he said if you don't then okay someone dies but with them what a coward and he lifted his middle and said up yours I quit.

Robert Stuverx the stepfather of the boys did not turn out he quit.

Now Stuart speies replaces this Robert Stuverx after Tom Phillips had refused sighting that the drill did not match him he had 3 girls and the drill has 3 boys that means his reactions might not be as perfect as it would be if he had boys so he talked to Stuart Speies who agree only because there was no other option.

Stuart speies now taking part in the drills with the kids

Stuart speies died in a cave in Arizona HIS coordinates 089867890283456789012347890126789012387890284089023879018678903856870
He said if I can then I can but what about the children then argued that the fbi had refused to pay him his money until the fbi on hearing this in front of everyone sent him instead of the father [step father] who ran away so from its start series.
Pc asert said I heard Robert run away from his duties towards his family that means that we need a replacement why not use this Stuart speies who keeps complaining and turn drill into live and just change satellite coordinates to Arizona town instead of desert that way what happens here means we were not in the desert and by the time God [he laughed] and said imagine if there was a God and us literally killing other people's kids to correct a wrong that could be so wrong he would simply say go to hell all of you imagine the people that would destroy from president who sign these drills to top fbi then he would kill everyone except Stuart speies the gentle honesty guy who can't do wrong then he would have to ask everyone what happened to him that he can't open his account with a life savings as he put

it then he would know about the lottery the child sacrifice and the killings of women and children of those who perish under the disguise of dolls but to cut on national insurance payouts to files instead of 200000 to his family these accounts are loaded with these monies now what case íkills all family members through drills the kids to be killed today are for the former worker so in three fùíí]

Pc atitap who said I can but who cover for me then he said what I am going to reveal is going to change the course of events from now on until everything is written in the books of creation for I have seen the lord so he removed his fake eye patch and said I can see but I can't hear but you keep making jokes about the fbi and they laughed then he said Stuart speies I heard he will go in I mean die tonight by 8pm

Pc action he said I can tell you for sure that he is going down if it was a joke before then he is not joking for I heard him order a real one than that baby sitting tiger but he said a friendly one

Pc abtinate said I want a Maneater for this coming drill but make it a bit hungry for this phase and make sure that I get to know who sent this one because if things are to get wrong I will say that I spoke to you about this meaning we never spoke

Pc atern he said I an nervous because the new guy might not react that can cost the children their lives whose these are by the way and he checked and cursed I am going there then he took his gun and left immediately and said fbi what are you up to these are very young kids your drills never took young lives what are you doing

Pc atter said I can but then kept quiet

Pc aertop said kids must not be part of this as this is against health and safety regulations article 58 that says no drills must

expose children if so a line leader Must be informed so who is the line leader?
Pc atop said if he can let there be someone for backup because if he doesn't shout that's it the animal is trained to respond to sound then he said I can but who will take over then asked what can be done in this situation then he was told to mitigate but saying I did do provide feedback and backup even if he had not done so
Pc aoll said I can if he can then said I provided back up but without the backup then say done he said done then an Atm approved then only one cop refused he said I want to if they can but given the situation I decided to decline and as per the rules if you are not happy then don't participate at all so I am going to walk then he walked but a scream tore the skies it's like the sitcom site with theater and chairs in one area and the real world on the other the when he had finished he said okay and walked back to his position and said I can if you can but what if we are to then what of the situation then he called in

Officer opqrstuvw and said I want to know why there is no back up to save those kids in case something goes wrong he said I put backup plan and everyone authorized it except Pc atoprstuvw who said I can but only with real back up plan then not with this I do I do but that put real humans at risk and instantly a huge shadow passed by his side and he literally shit himself and said I can but if he can then I can but this is not the way drills are done you provide the actual backup not just a tick then he said I think he can but then without the real backup then it is difficult to say what exactly happens there if a Maneater is hungry and you don't shout he will eat so test his shouting now but saying Maneater but he remained quiet and said it just

passed me a real Maneater maybe it's not as bad as it speed but we might just witness horror on tape then a small screen like that of a baby is all they heard then another small scream then a growling that died soon after and a scream then a real loud growling from the beast itself then a small scream that's all then they sat down to check project and he said looks pretty okay until the Maneater came out with a baby boy's head and growled before literally eat all his head then went back in and grabbed the other body and ripped the head off and said we can and we don't stand with the fbi he sacrifice children I want to file a report a one and one report and said write down that safety precaution has not be taken properly as such fbi is liable to compensation on the grounds of diminished responsibilities as it keeps loosing capacity to control itself from harm therefore must be held fully accountable to the following breaches
1. Child safety breached
2. People safety breached
3. Animal precautions not taken
4. Environmental safety not taken
5. Hope and balance not fully given
6. New balance not applied to this case
7. Wildlife prohibition during drills not adhered to
8. Animals with frenzy behavior are based
9. Housing accommodation for the kids without a father has not been requested meaning sacrifice because what you don't do is put kids at risk like they just did I quit the fbi today that could have been known prior to the start of the drill then he can prepare in advance then he sent for her and said you can do better than this

You can always say what can be done

After a long struggle of words then the fbi chief at the time said drills are meant to recreate situations that resemble real life dramas if to attract and interested party like the film industry who accounts for most of our donors as they and recreate scenarios we have dealt with and proved can be successfully handled out using wild animals but tonight you sacrificed these kids but why I want to know who is behind this because this can't be a coincidence no I refuse to believe that in fact if I want to be honest this is a manslaughter only without the court today you let down hard working men and women who protect innocent lives if you don't like me ask for a ballot box in fact I quit

Pc asert said I know sir there has been some screw up and now this is just the smoke screen so I quit too

Pc aoprt said I quit three expecting people to laugh but none laugh and sat down

Pc manop said I can quit today but I will stay we don't abandon the ship in the middle of the ocean when time comes I will quit

Pc asoft said I lost everything to the pandemic so I will stay

Pc avert said what could I have done better backup was not my region so I will stay I did my job right so I deny that I had something to do

God that job

Pc ateroppq said it can be done right next time and sat down he said I will and you promise to fulfill the drill requirements on time the question to ask is who did not do their job right this is the person to fall I did nothing wrong and can't take the blame for someone else because this won't solve the problem

At the end fbi lost 8 member of staff who quitted then the

matter was then real name aret Sanj.

Aret one I have to try and escape because I know that Maneater is around but then they said it's like last time nothing to worry about I wonder who is really behind this father why did you take your own life look how we are treated now like nothing and to make things worse we are no longer needed in their circle of trust they say we must not be part of them anymore buy mama took your best friend in Robert survex or suverx this guy at first he was the most serious guy I have ever met in my whole life until exactly two weeks ago when he said guys I am going to live your mother soon I want you to understand that you this had nothing g to do with you I am not wanted anymore these bastards after stealing our money for decades we are still broke they keep our money and now today someone told me what they do I know right now it's kinda creepy but you will believe here we go I work for the fbi and the fbi work for asert a company that murder politicians asert own banks and fbi collects funds for then so they have capital this is the catch fbi work just to collect and asert deals with the distribution that means all that money we have been talking about is not even fbis this is why fbi can't offer rewards never did and never will and as such we will be broke forever meaning I love mareena my push delicious candy pie come here hear this as well and I will tell you what you do today to get your parts for the premier of the movie once you are accepted you must say today we can't because our step dad Robert survex one asked what's the spelling again they all laughed but he said today I swear it's no laughing joke you enter and you are dead like your father and they all got upset but he said you will be upset if you don't listen marina translate as well in polish so that you remember

what to say mareena I beg you today go with them my love I marry you today to prove I am not running but if I go then there is never me okay so you must be there for the kids yes I agreed because I thought fbi have money fbi is just a useless killing machine but robby go with them what I know about movies [Mareena kliewsckies 089284689286789028768543210284109286285387189293821 09210 lives in gdnia Poland coordinates 0838689248789028367892138285789086481̄20]
If I could go with you then I would have but today if I go we all die if I don't show up they choose Tom phillips with his daughters then you guys you are safe whispering I had they want Tom dead as of yesterday he opened the pandora and took all his money he understood what the fbi failed to do with this task he accepted God and God told him the locker password its for his and he tried and it opened 4 billion and he ran away he was there if God was on earth he would here everything right now and tell everyone their passwords at the first meeting this is what happened he said looking at mareena caressing her fondly as if it's the last time we got together and asert said this is what we do we tell you a password you pick at random and you say I care all about passwords but not these this opens your passwords safe and then say a password you will remember forever and say this save forever and say it once then go but in 20 years use it to open your wealth
2077044 then he said then we were different people then new different life styles and now everything has changed if we Ask what you remembered then this is different now and if I Ask what is your password 20 years ago you probably didn't know but now you can see the frustration in everyone it was a one off

thing an experiment to test memory but now we have billions in these banks but the banks are for billionaires who has for all people and can easily know everyone's password kids if we don't go away this is last day officially we will leave on earth so he cried a0nd hugged them all and took mareena in the bedroom and said if i don't make it then the kids w0ill but to be on the safe side I won't go I will hide until this is over so know I will be there tonight but if things do not go according to plan then then know that I am okay because I will quit and go and work at the ranch today make sure that the kids are okay that the only important thing Tom phillips said i can but if you can then be there I have nothing to lose I am suspended anyway my kids are all girls so I have no

Tom phillips
I am tom phillips and I have nothing to worry about hard work pays I love life and life loves me the reason why fbi want me is to run fbi not to kill me as the only person to open my own safe after 20 the only one to do so after failing to find the human God the I am the best known replacement to te everyone their passwords the only reason why they need God because they have 8 tri[6] first password I ever used when I started this jog and it said [ ] and I transferred all to stomabelly who said
first everything in your stomabelly then ask what can be done with this wealth then he said deposit all into serth account when serth is dead take the money and deposit it all into erert and repeat the process but you must go in order of importance remove lower levels first before your higher cells then repeat the process until you are nearly at the top but to serve yourself empty your own into the highest that way you can wait for

others to clear theirs first before they can go for theirs first then aim higher by the time everyone realise what's going on they will be old without anything he cried and begged mareena to forgive him as he had promised her everything her ex couldn't the boy said it's okay I am cool with you I think you are the strongest I have met so far apart from running away today and he said today if I go seriously I will get all of you killed and I will hate to see that happening this is what will happen you go there and say we can this time because of step-dad is not there and girls are replacing us but it's all cool if you don't say it's all cool you will have lost they will put your dad's best friend to decide if you say its all cool he will know I send you to duck because today they try a new beast but this one removed the brain and passwords first because the word in the street is that fbi is broke if it's broke all the money they flash to us to get us hooked is not theirs they are like a security guard company that deliver cash for banks yes they can parade it but they are broke when fbi is broke it kills its on deliberately as a way of saying we broke we kill our own so don't go at all you hear and he said just okay but you not my dad right if he were here what would he be saying I think he would be like go but don't participate because danger today but I am like if you go Maneater is meant to feast on you live that's how fbi get the money through their job is just to collect money only if they don't have the money then how can they collect to collect they must have something going wrong for them to receive money when you are broke are you with me so I thought about it and said I can't die for nothing I am too proud to die for an organization like the broke fbi I love life I wanna wake up great and have everything I hate to wake up and say where is Jesus this is for fools so tomorrow

I am your dad and I say you are my son don't enter tomorrow or that you to Jesus okay arot. Aret and my number one ayot
Yes but no no no tomorrow if you want me in your life tomorrow say no okay mareena translate exactly again in polish language
Mareena [translated] tomorrow new daddy Roby ssid you say we can't enter without him so no at all okay.
Arot okay mammy my beautiful mama so daddy said we can't go tomorrow I don't want to go okay I tell my friends I am not dying yet and mareena ..who told you you are dying then he said everyone we talk to ghosts and angels and they said Maneater can talk he said I have to kill all and remove passwords stolen by roberts sturvex but he did not steal the passwords the money is in his locker he is the sturvex rob got his money and is running from us my got he got 4 billion dollars that's why fbi are putting real Maneater so you might and say I can't go then he wins if we go if he turns up and die then fbi will start manhunt and cover that he stole 4 billion actually asking the people to donate that kind of money to people they have never met or who literally don't touch the money a money collected iis dumped in huge vaults within fbi where only asert has keys meaning forever fbi poor and removing hard earned cash from the people on false account To the fbi asert is like God it removes excess money from the system and safe keeps it to keep the American dollar a dream without asert the economy would struggle but asert means no extra cash then rob said asert is the president of the United States working for God but without giving God his money that means not paying any taxes to avoid the 1776th revolution battle the forefathers established a system that collects what is

calculated as taxes for God meaning if God was on earth he would ask everyone to pay a percentage of their salary to him as taxes to service things that means the American people now free from the still owes God some form of tax system so instead of saying when he comes on earth we don't have to show their appreciation in helping them write their constitution asert representing God's representative collects taxes on behalf of God that means money in this account belong to anyone who declares to be God's representative on earth within 60 days of being appointed by God on American soil home or abroad as in article 38 of the constitution of the federation of American people articles of 1888 the constitution still in operation today if that person exist then he must tell the president of the United States in any way within that time frame to have access to that asert account he has the password already his date of birth must match the American independence minus God times which is 6 days that means 28 of June 1976 Elon musk and David gomadza are the God's born on 28 of June hence the owners of asert account current value $....

David Gomadza under the constitution article 38 is the president of the United States of America by abode and by adoption which can be facilitated by residents or marriage or on boarding an empty vessel

Ayot if I can today I just want to sleep and eat because I am that lazy as if I die today and it's like what for then I saw something that worries me the most a maneater over the other side looking and searching for something that freaked me I just said aah what's this and looked at him but he disappeared I said God protect us because Maneater love humans but I think if my real dad was here he could not even tried anything but me being me I think we could have been easily saved. A large scream could have alerted others that we needed time and help they could have blocked a section to let us out because it is manmade park

Ayet

I can kill it if it comes near me I am a big boy but if it's too much I self terminate after knowing how my father killed himself

Stuart speies

I can but what about the children if I can I can but then again I can't believe they put a man eater on a drill I think chances are that we might end up being eaten alive this is wrong I never had a drill with a man eater before aty what can be done in this situation

1. You can call someone now for help just text hel.p
2. You can always say onerous
3. You can admit you can't fight it and surrender but then it must tear you so you won't forget forever
4. You can say HELP! loudest Maneater gets scared often runs away but if no help arrive will tear you before help arrives
5. Will attack fast and preserve you to keep you but not each for being like a God

You mean alive? I hear others talking about it

6. He will talk literally talk if scared of being killed after that
7. Will ask questions about you
8. Will eat you fast and ask what can be done
9. Will check if everything is okay
10 will ask for help to kill you

I am aty Australian type established on 23 may 1968 which is his birthday and I am designed to kill men who jump and then run away before they are killed these we call renegades because they are supposed to be killed yet they don't die his father was stubborn took 28 years to kill because he always asked what can be done all the time and always pick the first choice until some noticed and started the shuffling first that means the first one was never the best choice until the day he died but his son has learnt to read all options hence now I am partnered with the American

asm now what can we do is that if we combine we can become lethal to him the use are very defensive so I use that as my own defense against him and let aty become the attacking one's Australia's are the more aggressive ones and ruthless ones with all rotational tricks. Read your last log file I aty ser387890 is going to kill Stuart speies on 25 April 2023 and today's date is 19 June 1968 its his birthday. How I don't know but death is just a needle away I have a deadly muscle paralyser there can ever be code 0898382867890 and the antidote is binaryreversex1billiononly if you say forever it won't work Stuart speiss continued

If I am attacked then what should I do just say hellono hello no x28

But if spared but the kids attacked then jump on it very hard and scream loudest panicked freezes and shout okkillx28 then run hardest before cramp undoes but you can start by asking it whatthefuck x 28

Thenwhyx28 thenwhatcanbedonex28

In doing all this you make the Maneater change priorities by asking other critical questions if I go without being attacked can I leave? Yes but always say run run run x8 that means every one must escape first before you if you stop then all die without shouting the above what yes you freeze they all freeze and all dies he looked lost and said if I die who else automatically dies with me

Ayet

Ayot

Aret

All yes guardians are better than fathers and must always be followed run now before Maneater comes they all run you stand they all stand okay then program run don't stand but run
Programrunbinaryreversedissipsteforever
Programrundissipateallexternallinksforever
Programrunquarantineeverythingfromoutsideinoutsidevaultwhichyoumustcreatealso
Programruncreateoutsidebodyskysuspendedvaulttoreceiveallcodesfromothersoutdidemysystem
Progranrunblockallcodeswithsourceasearth
Programblockandordisableallswitchesinadvanceforever

If I Ask what are my options then this is the answer
1. to die today
2. To live then die
3. To live react then die
4. To ask die
5. To die fie
6. To ask then die anyway
7. To injure then die
8. To ask die then die
9. To use then die
10. To die then die again

Before he finished the man eater pounced on him and he died

long ago log calculated at 22.09 as
Breath 78
Ast 10
Aso 9
Ata 26
Ama 10
Ata 7
Aro 3
Ava 8
Adt 7
Aot 6
Aao 2
That means he panicked first and froze which is against the human predefined system

Stuart speies
Current coordinates are
089789867890283698789028468789028918486789028411384
At the cave in Arizona above coordinates now skeleton and skull pierced top left side and hide opening left side his cell number is 08789028387654386 but working just made a call to a number in california1

089789867890283698789028468789028918486789028411384
It's Stuart speies who died on 25 April 2023 instead if the target Tom phillips currently at coordinates
089878678902348902878902841023867890486185280120
Arizona restaurant

Robert Spurvex narrating his account of events

i am tom and i died so early it hurts on 25 of april 2023 i said what can be done then i said if i can what about the children then said if you can then i can then went out of the room i was with maureena who said what about my kids you want to play games with the fbi they can get our kids killed you know but she said i can but then what you are on your own then i take the kids once the money is out then i said from who and he said from all but the fbi they don't give and never paid a penny on rewards but i can ask if that changed then she looked at me and said okay then she left but came back and said what can be done but then i said i want to ask what is to be of all these money games with the fbi she said what if we get the money babe that will solve all our problems so go on the run with the kids and bring them back in late 2023 this was january 2023 then i took the kids and went with them but no one saw us for months but we were local then one day i received a tip that said i must hide for another 3 months then 8 more then 10 more until i am tired and said that's it kids let's go and get ready for punishment then this night a lot of things happened a cat died in front of us i searched it for a tag but it literally said i got killed by the fbi Í another thing is the arrival of a hyena that said i tired then another said i run why then another that said i kill you

Tom Phillips

I am the real Tom Phillips but I did not die that day 25 April 2023 when the kids of robert speies were killed.

Stuart Speies.

A large growling startled us and i panicked and took the kids then we left but he said i want to eat i mean one of them and i said okay then i grabbed a fruit and said okay then put one down then a huge growling sound outside shook all of us and i literally squirt a little shit the other until a huge mountain lion just grabbed the kid and shock him so hard he broke in its grin and something fell down my heart stopped literally and i fell down the next thing animal detected growling.

Maneater thinking.
i eat i want free food i smell from afar and track nice fresh smell here so i say i check maybe guns and i run but if not eat fresh food

Stuart Speies

then when i woke up the kids were gone one was torn in two but half moving and i said eat me not the kids then he ran away and not to be seen but i thought the two kids could be alive so i tried to trail it hesitating then i saw an arm of my son and i cried then a hand then a torso of the other then i sat down crying helplessly and [calculate DNA sequence to get more information] xxtrtuvwxyzrtuvwxyzstuyvxyzssrtuv child chromosomes a boy aged 8 years old dead no electromagnetic waves at all unless faked because has markings around it of yellow then the lion grabbed me from behind then eat me starting with the back and then my neck and i only said god then died long ago started at 22.08 pm in arizona desert just between lounge and mile where the distance is 180 degrees from each other but below ground level he growled when it inserted its teeth into his skull oh god i died today 25 of april 2023 for my mistakes i got the kids killed but was supposed to be a money scheme gone wrong maybe fbi themselves playing with kids lives but what can i say i am the one responsible for their safety and who thought a mountain lion can do this but it did i had never been so close to one but they are big where is my heard but how i can speak and when i looked around a huge figure sat in the gold chair and said what are you talking about i am Yahweh and they all smiled with huge faces 10 times normal human being and said did i get smaller but the woman said what if but then and stopped the huge old faced man said can i but then he said i can but then they are all dead so what the point but then and all looked around and said what can be done but then the big one rose and left drfting like a huge gasoline tractor then all followed it and i was since ever here.

8928378900028678902848789028467890284789902851836789018 4286789028678902489018326789 01
god i died i was tricked to run with the kids then we all died a mountain lion tear us up into pieces my two kids first then me then when i was about to die my other son who came to me running then i heard a large noise then when i looked he was bleeding badly he said daddy look this eat me and died long ago for the last boy finished at 22.36pm in a cave at arizona camping site coordinates 862848386789028418286789028419023678901234567890
my name is trinka i died on 25 april at 22.37pm in cave some huge animal took aret first then arot then dead left and came back carrying baby aret then arot half all then sat down and said god i killed my own kids for money i want to die too god said okay you too
i am god i am police officer eret-eres sstuvw real name astopman stuvwer and said if i can play their game who can i be and he said god i want to know what brings you to the desert and why you run with the children before our own lion from the zoo eats you then he said what it's a zoo lion then stop it shoot it i give up i go back to my wife maureena and my daughter but he said we have already calculated that this case if nurtured will bring in a lot of money three kids mixed race can bring in millions in revenue from our partner companies who donate as early as weeks after their disappearance and into 20 years of the case being open now what is that you want you have no pension so what can we do but kill all family its a job but someone must do it now what can be said of people who want to

play god with kids they can't keep
arizona check on the web is the most dangerous place to be with kids he wants to die said one pc to the other pc atop ator real name tomas zucker who said let them go back before things gets out of control but he said they were not supposed to go into a cave he was told recall tell him again never to enter the cave or this drill8367890 will end up dreaded as hell and might bring all of us down one laughed how will they know they have to bring god in first then try to figure out everything we are gay lover but cops if any ask we do each other in the woods if not then we ask what can be done then this is the end of life 3 precious lost today but what can be learnt from all this this is a fatal mistake ajy must have warned them and ask said we could have saved these but it's a learning curve now call the fbi hazard prevention and say we lost all to a mountain lion and bring drill 2 to investigate while we clean their bodies okay then he left and i got up and aimed at our lion we call tiger in case others are listening and i missed that sends panicked at it target pc arestop who said dam it what can be done but he said walla and it stopped [walla walla what can i stop but i can't kill and stop o must eat the little i hide first to remove brain so that no human read nor god read then it welled and left then written chewing but said i can't eat all so can i eat the head only got to hide the others deep into the cave,] and left then returned and growled before it left
the other man came to collect the bodies and quickly collect the first son aret then left then collected arot the came back with the other baby and said there are people coming this way so holding half the torso then he said can we wait until they have gone and they hid in the cave but the lion returned and dragged officer aresteps then the other lion and ran away into t0he woods but i thought you shot it with a dart then he looked for it silently knowing it will be eating this pc but he found him sat down but dead and said what are you doing but he said i died long ago calculated at 22.48pm on 25 april 2023 as

it turns out it was his atm

i am atm advanced human machine developed by aster system california firm to explore the possibility of a god on earth but then they started faking everything until 2020 someone claims to have decoded god from britain but blanket put in place by asertop of bradford as mental health i am pc aretopes of the california death squad we came here to kill tom phillips and his sons for deception and to prove that there still no god

of course the children will remember when he fell lions like human brains a lot we did research that says every lion will always eat first an adult human brain so nothing to read here for all those who are clever but if we can ask what can be of all these when it comes to running away with own kids to trick the fbi then this is the answer they all die a real death this as to stop them doing it again ahhuh [laughing] but if god is listening his auditorium has been eaten so how can he talk git has created a human being that is so clever we must appreciate but we have a lot to learn we must act fast and get what we need

pc arestopes said if i can then what but instantly a wave froze all unknown and

pc asyopers said thinking who is tom phillips if i can ask but we don't. care we want to blow his head if the tiger misses him and his children

pc aterpst real name mopx tyon said what can be done but then froze then thinking he said what can be of fathers who really don't like their kids enough and sacrifice them for literally 80 000 dollars this is sad i love you chris i love you troy i am not this man and the grabbed a ring on his neck and kissed it

pc asertopqrst uvwxyz meaning atopqrt real name stopqrs said thinking what is to be can be but then again this is life he took the chance but took too long and now the death squads is here to finish them off day 25 april 2023 there can never be another day for your family but a new billion dollar case for us as it stand globally we have 8 trillion dollars among all global force to fight dg when the shit happens but what if the decrees don't materialise

pc asser who just moved from jamaica said i know nothing what this is all about i just spliff when they group i go but then again did anyone see that lion i am like is it for real i froze my balls still shaking but americans crazy if effects bigup i just thought what about the kids

pc asertopqrstuvw real name tom phillips i am tom phillips and i an a cop this drill is out of the blue i am the real tom phillips but fbi replaced me with ajern stern meaning imposter but he looks just like me but he died fir real as i heard but his name is sealed in a bank account where no human has access to now what is with this all game my kids got killed though but i died too but its a job i have transfer to switzerland

pc asertop real name mineop said who is who can but me then volunteered to play tom phillips but in the build up to this drill he discovered that the dangers were real with him questioning everything for example who did that in front of a kid is this a drill or you want us to be killed that growling is frightening please retract from being excessive the kids thought it was a joke but one literally shits itself mind the kids only i am a hero but this is wrong this animal is real they say tiger but it's lion if lion it's untamable then what i have no gun they stripped me of everything my gun and knife but one kid stole a knife so we could be good but i never shit myself but today i did so watch it aty are they trying to kill me yes you volunteered so anything can happen but what can be done if it's like this just say hurry up bitches so they kill you fast what i thought it's a drill it is but the last in series is or ends in death i calculated already your long ago

vitals 36

asat 29
at 76
as 7
able 22
ahs 4
ass 3
aop 7
aon 3
aht 10
aso 8
aaa 2

so if it happens that you die at death reception say i have everything ready so you go straight to god olay but he remained quiet instantly the huge lion stood at the entrance and he shit himself and when a person shit himself all actions are frozen but it was triggered by a code 89286789028367890284190678902843867890 that he froze when he could have screamed as on rehearsals but it went straight for the little cute boy and grabbed him by the stomach and violently shook him that he literally U off into two and dropped down instead of known reaction of running away with food it dropped both pieces now red faced as in the eyes of aty [australian volunteer] then he came back for the other boy and removed head and ran away without a scream then it instantly came back by this time the father [actor] immobilized by sitting himself ran to check status bringing back the bottom halves if we ask why he could not find the top parts then instantly the lion stood at the door and stooped in front and pushed him so hard that something literally broke down and it eat his back as instructed at rehearsal through this code eat man hipbone and remove aty and hide it in a cave close by and remove all brain and eat after tell the brain in your stomach to convert all the information into mirror images that depict war but fall down all then it did now as it raised him another man stood at the door and it chased after him as he ran screaming walla walla then it stopped and its own atm translated the words to human meaning just a drill don't hurt anymore but it looked and another code 82386789028418902867890386789028386789 arrived and it quickly went back and took ate the remaining boy removing all intestines and pulling the neck out to reveal a long trunk of the boy and lay down eating him and growled and started sniffing the father and said what can i eat' all today but then and then what all humans can do is look then i go and hide and eat all tonight then footsteps outside panicked it that it looked wobbly and lay down breathing hard

pc omnopqrstuv real name stopquarstuhh said if all humans can eat everything then all animals can eat everything and run to their owners and whispered who is the owner of that animal then he said a zoo in britain known as chester zoo and this animal is meant to have gone there what does that mean the fbi hide incrementing park so that only god can know this but he will need passwords to-do this but then again if he can get the passwords then who can get what then stopped

kid 1 aret age 7 said real dad do you copy stepfather shit himself and froze in front of tiger but hhee it's hungry maneater ohh he took arot and tore him is this real daddy come daddy come it's real i to die too atm say i finish you all as tge bet says who can wipe all family and get all killed for 80 000 dollars which the fbi will never realise to the public but donate to their housing association but god we here is in england and black to save us all but the kids please god that man they call dg is fake he stole from me his brain and he wants his back but what can he do they killed his daughter through a stroke of pen go left when they mean right and she died crying daddy daddy daddy and the girlfriend only said where are you come please please and don't let our daughter die please but the nurse sacked so hard that she broke instantly when something breaks forever it can never heal and

said what is to be could be they might all break after this
arot said what is to be can be then stopped before the lion ate him
pc asert said what happened to the kids and cried silently and said
god i swear i have knotting to do with the deaths of the kids and die
being torn apart saying i am strong but i die so what is strong i was
not supposed to die they changed the maneater this one is aggressive
and i am in half can i walk again mummy why you don't love us sure
you have beautiful
kids you borrow another husband like dad it's wrong i i i i i i i
god i died because some thing i never see before eat me into two but
thank you god i can walk i have legs but not human legs i am like a
duck so did i die am i alive or what happened my heard is so
confused is this your dream or my dream that maneater tore me apart
so what is this i still feel his grip one in my skull the other on my
right stomabelly and he talk though he said i eat today but what
about and looked at dad while he cry like a baby plus the only good
thing out of this is that he is not my real dad they changed but he
refused to talk he said he is ajex a death squad member with the fbi
but i wish my daddy was there he could have saved us but he died
first so i heard by him when i was about to be eaten i said why you
don't move like my daddy he could have screamed to chase him
away first you so quiet so he come in why he said shock your daddy
died first and i said what so i touch by belly button and said over
where at maneater to eat us all you where tell me right now i can feel
you crying like a bitch on heat now i know who the bitch on heat is
it's not maureen my beautiful push mama but you you you you you
you you uou you you x 179284186 i kill myself before he grab me
and he froze before maneater grabbed him and shock him so
violently that he broke into two to show rage as a reason why the
step father did not act but as it turns out pc aertopqrst real name
asuvwo sent him the all muscle clipper code 8428678690 that froze
him only his brain was fully awake that he kept shitting himself until

the lion attacked him that was the lion won't eat him but preserve him in a cave foreternity because he is sacred he did not move or fear him this is the father of the boys they will find after 20 years decomposed and unrecognisable but in good shape as he has just been digitally mummified frozen all muscles clapped together we can see that only one kid is left standing as the master of ceremony to close this round of never seen before events he said silently i don't call a coward your own kids you trust them with another bitch ass man he confessed he is gay and don't want mama so who does he want you i guess now but you sounded the most strong daddy in the world championing us yet this lookalike bitch us motherfucker senorita puking guts dance daddy and the smell surely is to upset the maneater the way he shook little aret is terrible god don't forgive you if he does i will never honor you again it's my turn and what kind of maneater who can speak he said if i keep then tomorrow i might just lay in this nino and he said god i am the last standing because everyone panicked i tried to copy this fool and all my little brother are dead no point playing hero big bro plus i have no chance the maneater seemed so ruthless i swear they did not feed him for a long time and oh my god he bite me oh this is it i thought i can walk out of this but i died calculating long ago so i keep hearing and it said long ago calculated at 22.53pm on 25 april 2023 death at and i fly i swear i never thought i can fly and reached a huge ground with ice only that slides but don't move and i said jesus where but no one answer they all said who is jesus this is the reception can you all move forward and i looked i calculated 879678396 people in front of asking something that kept saying i won but i died as well as him so everything is a lie i should have defended him and warned him for we both died him first at 22.58pm on 25 april 2023 and me at 23.08 pm 25 april 2023 after reading the longest boring long ago close even now i don't even know what it's all about it it reads
i can say that my mission is to protect this family but for only our

interest this family tricked fbi that they can mind read and we gave them 80000 in advance for house indirectly by making deals with the housing association then they refused to take out a target assigned to them a robot if you like that don't move but they refused and said that is fbi work but today i said get the job done or i put death squad on you but he said a am a good cop i can find a bad cop who can do this but i have guts to run from trouble to save my family all he has to do is scream maneaters are afraid of the noise and my boys are okay after 8 years i collect the reward money for the best daddy in the world price when fbi finds the kids safe and sound then call us to ask what can be done then this is the answer the fbi can always get people hooked to their money and if we are fair then the fbi has a responsibility to protect the kids by putting safe systems at work their drills always ends up in deaths is this deliberate or real
the end
reception for aret died 25 april 2023 he came in two to us but one to himself and we mended him together using benzole actyte then he cried for days then he said where is jesus but he refused to speak to him and said okay what about his father but fathers around the world have failed us so i can but only because i lost faith in fathers then he said can i walk it's like i am kinda mended now i now can see human legs are they mine but i am way smaller than before who change us into this small then he looked shocked to see what god looked like with 8 heads why does he need so many heads that's why he can't help anyone they quarrel all the time right? never-ending god i am here because i got killed by a maneater who eat me and tore me but i am clever i was already this is because he tore me after the death code then he looked at me and said stay in reception forever i have no powers to send him for rebirth but my representative has powers the code is 892807890286780284 he can only say send him for rebirth back to earth for eternity so he don't die easily again as death tends to follow death

the court dismiss this case on merit and write a verdict of and he stopped and said the fbi are behind this and they walk make a note that the fbi are responsible for his death as they should have looked at safe systems at work but to release him back then sent him back asap he got up and went and they said when he come he will send you and i am still here who is this person to come.
the end.

STUART SPEIES

God I come in peace I feel robbed for the hard work I put in and now taken by the fbi who as of today owed me 4867890 but I ignored their threats that if you keep asking for money then someone who can will go and get the money but.

[MAREENA KLIEWSCKIES

[mareena kliewsckies
08928468928678902876854321028410928628538718929382109210 lives in gdnia poland coordinates
08386892487890283678921382857890864 8120]
if i could go with you then i would have but today if i go we all die if i don't show up they choose tom phillips with his daughters then you guys you are safe whispering i had they want tom dead as of yesterday he opened the pandora and took all his money he understood what the fbi failed to do with this task he accepted god and god told him the locker password

According to mareena 4 of my children died that day trinka. Ayet. Ayot Aret 3 boys and 1 girl.
I am trinka I am a girl aged 10 years old but have different father to the boys I am white my mother is mareena the gorgeous push lady as people call her how did you die a man came and said go in as well all your brothers are waiting for you and I was excited to appear on television so I ran there and there was no one it was in the middle of the woods and something talk I swear and said who sent you I never

eat meat for females my name is arosetertp the lion king from Chester zoo in England I collect passwords for a company called asert in Britain run secretly by Barclay's Bank and the queen not sure no0w the queen is over I mean dead ryoinlanguage as they call it in England and it said go back you are not needed I smell no passwords in you unless you want to die too with your brothers so I said they never die why they die hey they are my brothers and they said they will be on television acting but dead [I not understand complicated language I learn basic and this translate 08983890287890684 8210 advanced rotary system Mitsubishi] then I went back but the first man had gone and the second man said why have you come back go your brothers are waiting for you I refused because Maneater said I give only one chance if you come back that means you want to be eaten so he grabbed my hand and dragged me saying I told you it's only a drill

But he stopped and said what did you say I said leave me alone or fbi kill you and he laughed and said I am fbi so go back in there so I cried and my heard was biten and he [maneater] said I warned you one chance and you die he removed my head

1. Pc rtopqrestuvw meaning stopquvw meaning aretuvw meaning soroq Pc soroq
2. Fbi
3.

Aret died 25 April 2023 at drill site in Arizona area owned by Barclays Bank as for research and developemnt he is still at same place coordinates 08983678902841 9867890 in a cave

THE KILLER, THE CONFESSIONS AND THE COORDINATES

The killer is the main eater currently at Chester zoo in Britain

stuart speies
current coordinates are
08978986789028369878902846878902891848678902841384
at the cave in arizona above coordinates now skeleton and skull

pierced top left side and hide opening left side his cell number is 08789028387654386 but working just made a call to a number in california1
08978986789028369878902846878902891848678902841384
it's stuart speies who died on 25 april 2023 instead if the target tom phillips currently at coordinates 08987867890234890287890284102386789048618528012 0 arizona restaurant

Fbi caused the death of stuart speies by neglecting safety and standards procedures on the last 8 drills before that he is still in this cave its owned by a joint venture between the queen and a bank used to be called worcester bank that was bought by barclays bank but ever since nothing has happened to the accounts now with value over 8 trillion dollars but account asert is for God's representative on earth as taxes in advance to the owner of the land plus his commission according to article 38 of the original chater of the American constitution signed on 28 of June 1776 meaning the asert is a person born on this day who meet all the characteristic and is a patriot of America home or abroad because this is the only way to guarantee the America dream as in the process America inherit the untransferable decrees with total value of 489 trillion dollars

My name is David Gomadza I was born on 28 of June 1976
I am Yahweh [God] 's perfect mirror image on earth as I founded Tomorrow's World Order making me the first global president meaning of all the world just like of all and heaven
I am Yahweh's Representative on earth authorized and licensed
I have signed [authorized and licensed] decrees
This is my ask
Ask.davidgomadzaauthorised.licensed.checkya.askya.ya

https://find-and-update.company-information.service.gov.uk/company/12326946

…I found God…visit www.twofuture.world

How To Find All Missing Persons / Unsolved Cases. And
Collect All Reward Offers. Volume XXXIX. THE CASE OF STUART SPEIES
WHO SWAPPED WITH TOM PHILLIPS

THE CLAIM

the reward offer

THE COLLECTION

www.twofuture.world/donate

ABOUT DAVID GOMADZA

visit www.twofuture.world

signed david gomadza
ask.davidgomadzaauthorised.licensed.checkya.askya.ya

14 June 2024 17.56 pm
scotland
00447719210295
davidgomadza@hotmail.com
info@twofuture.world

www.ingramcontent.com/pod-product-compliance
Lightning Source LLC
Chambersburg PA
CBHW030513220526
45464CB00006B/2775